THE STORMY SOUTHERN OCEAN

Doreen Gonzales

Enslow Elementary

an imprint of

Enslow Publishers, Inc.

40 Industrial Road
Box 398
Berkeley Heights, NJ 07922
USA

http://www.enslow.com

Enslow Elementary, an imprint of Enslow Publishers, Inc.

Enslow Elementary is a registered trademark of Enslow Publishers, Inc.

Library of Congress Cataloging-in-Publication Data:

Gonzales, Doreen.
   The stormy southern ocean / Doreen Gonzales.
      p. cm. — (Our earth's oceans)
   Includes index.
   Summary: "Learn about the Southern Ocean—the animals that call it home, the seafloor, and all its resources. Also
     read about the people who have explored it and what is being done to keep the Southern Ocean clean"—Provided
     by publisher.
   ISBN 978-0-7660-4091-5
   1. Antarctic Ocean—Juvenile literature. I. Title.
   GC461.G67 2013
   551.46'17—dc23   2012007616

Future editions:
Paperback ISBN 978-1-4644-0149-7
ePUB ISBN 978-1-4645-1056-4
Single-User PDF ISBN 978-1-4646-1056-1
Multi-User PDF ISBN 978-0-7660-4434-0

Printed in the United States of America

102012 Lake Book Manufacturing, Inc., Melrose Park, IL

10 9 8 7 6 5 4 3 2 1

To Our Readers: We have done our best to make sure all Internet Addresses in this book were active
and appropriate when we went to press. However, the author and the publisher have no control over and
assume no liability for the material available on those Internet sites or on other Web sites they may link to.
Any comments or suggestions can be sent by e-mail to comments@enslow.com or to the address on the
back cover.

♻ Enslow Publishers, Inc., is committed to printing our books on recycled paper. The paper in every book
contains 10% to 30% post-consumer waste (PCW). The cover board on the outside of each book contains
100% PCW. Our goal is to do our part to help young people and the environment too!

Table of *Table of* CONTENTS

The Southern Ocean borders Antarctica. The area it covers used to be considered parts of the Atlantic, Pacific, and Indian Oceans. The blue circle shows the path of the Antarctic circumpolar current.

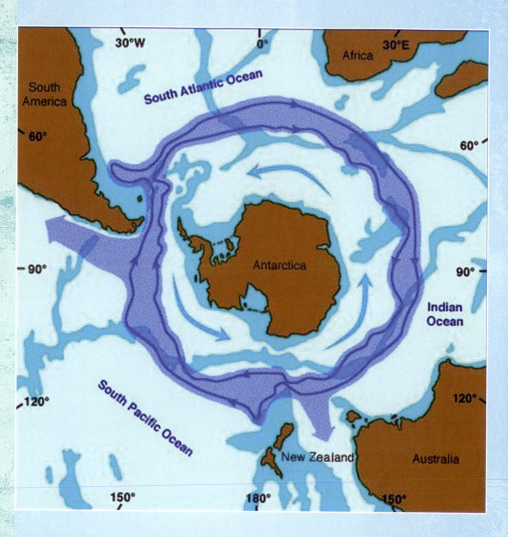

THE OCEAN *at the* BOTTOM *of* *the* WORLD

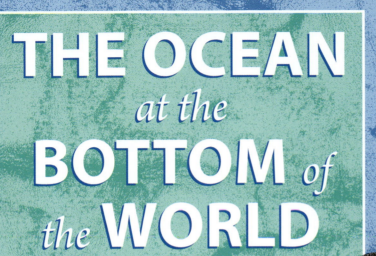

The Southern Ocean is the
newest ocean in the world. This is not
because its waters have just appeared.
It is because boundary lines for other
oceans were changed. This
created a new ocean. The Southern
Ocean became an ocean in 2000.

The Southern Ocean surrounds the
continent of Antarctica. It begins along
the coast of Antarctica and extends
north to 60° south latitude.

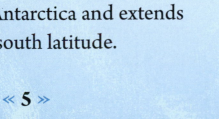

The Southern Ocean is small. It covers about 7.8 million square miles (20,327,000 million square kilometers).

The Circumpolar Ocean

The Southern Ocean is different from every other ocean. It surrounds a continent and makes a ring around the globe.

The Southern is also unique because it sits at the southern end of the earth around the South Pole. This makes it a polar ocean.

Because the Southern Ocean is both circular and polar, it is called circumpolar. Being circumpolar makes the Southern's climate and life different from any other ocean.

Polar regions are tilted toward the sun for almost half the year. During this time the sun shines for twenty-four hours each day. For the other half of the year, polar regions are tilted away from the sun. During these times it stays dark for twenty-four hours a day.

Sea Ice

The air above the Southern Ocean is always cold. Its waters are cold, too. Their temperatures are usually about 28°F (−2°C).

Much of the water in the Southern Ocean is frozen. Frozen seawater is called sea ice. Sea ice covers over one million square miles (2.6 million square kilometers) of the Southern all year long. Most of it extends northward from Antarctica.

Blood Falls seeps from the end of the Taylor Glacier. Scientists believe a buried saltwater reservoir is partly responsible for the red color, which is a form of iron.

Southern Ocean sea ice grows in the winter. It can increase by 2.5 miles (4 kilometers) each day. During the coldest part of the year, it covers six times more area than it does in the summer.

Yet even in the winter there is open water in the Southern. Most of it is at the far northern edge of the ocean.

Icebergs

Antarctica is covered with a layer of ice called a glacier. Sometimes pieces of it break off and fall into the sea. These pieces are called icebergs.

Icebergs are parts of the polar ice cap that have broken off and fallen into the sea. This iceberg is floating in the Gerlache Strait on the west side of Antarctica.

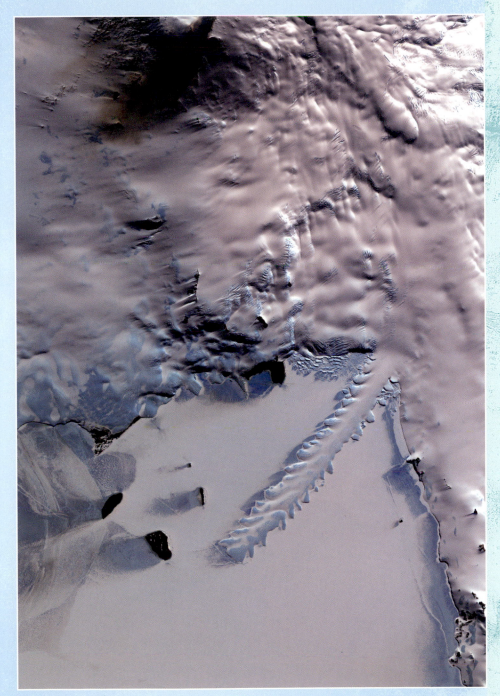

The Erebus glacier in Antarctica sticks out off the coast of Ross Island. It forms a long ice tongue, a long and narrow sheet of ice sticking out from the coastline.

The Southern Ocean is full of icebergs from Antarctica.

Icebergs can be almost one thousand feet (three hundred meters) thick. Yet only a small part of any iceberg is seen above the ocean. The biggest part lies below the surface.

Known as the "great ocean conveyor," the Antarctic circumpolar current is very important in understanding the world's climate. This current carries water, heat, and more to the Atlantic, Indian, and Pacific oceans.

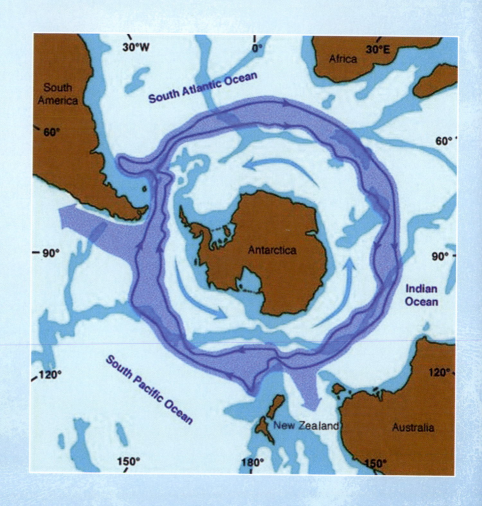

Icebergs can be clear, white, or blue. Some icebergs have rocks or plants inside them. These rocks or plants can color the icebergs green, brown, or pink.

Winds and Currents

Strong winds blow over the Southern Ocean. These winds create waves nearly 20 feet (6 meters) high.

One wind creates the Antarctic circumpolar current. A current is a body of water that moves in a regular and constant motion. It is like a river in the sea.

The Antarctic circumpolar current is the world's largest current. It circles Antarctica, moving around the entire globe with no land to stop it.

Chapter 2

OCEAN RESOURCES

The continent of Antarctica is an unusual place. It is not divided into countries. Nor is it owned by any one country. No one lives on Antarctica permanently, and there are no cities there. People all over the world want to keep the land and water there as natural as possible. They have encouraged countries to work together to protect Antarctica and the Southern Ocean.

In 1959, many countries signed a treaty about the polar area. The agreement was a list of rules about what could be done on Antarctica and in the Southern Ocean. By signing the treaty, the nations agreed to leave most of the resources there untouched.

Oil and Gas

Scientists believe that oil and gas lie below the seafloor. These fuels could be used by all kinds of machines. Tons of sand and gravel also lie at the

This Weddell seal wears a video data recorder that scientists use to create a 3-D map of its movement in the water as it hunts for prey. Researchers hope to learn more about the seals' hunting behavior during the darkness in late winter.

bottom of the ocean. The Southern Ocean may hold enormous quantities of other valuable resources. However, because of the treaty, none of these resources will be taken from the sea anytime soon.

Marine Life

The Southern Ocean is full of life, and some fishing is allowed there. Most fishing is done on big ships that have large crews. Krill is the most popular catch. Krill are small shrimp-like animals. They are mostly used for animal feed.

Whales, seals, penguins, and seabirds are also abundant in Southern waters. However, most countries have agreed not to hunt these animals. These agreements are another way of keeping the Antarctic region as natural as possible.

The Southern Ocean as a Science Laboratory

The Southern Ocean is one of the most unusual places on earth. This makes it an exciting place for scientists to study. Although there are no cities

· OCEAN RESOURCES ·

Krill is the main catch of the few countries that operate fishing vessels in the Southern Ocean. Krill is also the main food for many marine animals, such as penguins and whales.

on Antarctica, there are several research stations. Twenty-nine different countries have built research stations there. Added together, almost 5,000 people stay at these stations. They come to study the wildlife, climate, and unique conditions.

Oceanographers are researching how plants and animals work together to survive in the

A U.S. Antarctic Program participant stands a safe distance away from two Weddell seals. The Antarctic Treaty forbids directly touching wild animals unless the person has a scientific permit.

extreme conditions of the Southern Ocean. They are also looking to the ocean for clues about how the earth is changing.

In addition, thousands of tourists visit the Southern Ocean each year. They come to see its fantastic icebergs and spectacular ocean life.

THE TERRAIN

The Southern Ocean is not flat on the bottom. It has many features such as a continental shelf, basins, and trenches.

The Land Under the Ocean

The bottom of the ocean slopes gently as it moves away from Antarctica toward the deep sea. This gently sloping bottom is called a continental

shelf. The Southern Ocean's continental shelf ends at depths of about 1,300 feet (400 meters). This is deeper than the continental shelves of most other oceans.

At the end of the continental shelf, the seafloor drops sharply. This steep drop is called the continental slope. The floor of the deep sea is at the bottom of the slope. The floor of the

An octopus rests on the floor of McMurdo Sound.

Southern Ocean is about 15,000 feet (4,500 meters) below the ocean surface.

Several basins lie at the bottom of the Southern. A basin is a wide flat area on the seafloor. The Southern holds three major basins.

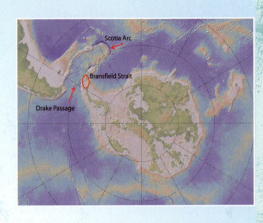

Scotia Arc

Bransfield Strait

Drake Passage

Bransfield Strait, Drake Passage, and Scotia Arc (South Sandwich Islands) lie between Antarctica and South America.

Mountains

Two main mountain ranges run along the bottom of the Southern Ocean. They are often called ridges. The first is the Scotia Arc. It runs north of the Antarctic Peninsula. The second is the Pacific-Antarctic Ridge. This ridge is a small part of a long mountain range called the mid-ocean ridge. The mid-ocean ridge runs through every ocean on earth.

Trenches

There are also many trenches in the Southern Ocean. A trench is a deep, narrow channel that cuts through the ocean floor.

Hook Ridge

Orca Vol.

Three Sisters

Lined up along the floor of the Southern Ocean are Hook Ridge, Orca Volcano, and Three Sisters, which have been recently volcanically active.

The deepest point in the Southern Ocean lies at the bottom of the South Sandwich Trench. This point is more than 23,000 feet (7,000 meters) below the ocean's surface.

Above the Surface

Sea ice covers much of the Southern Ocean all year long. In some places, it is 6.5 feet (2 meters) thick.

Seawater freezes at a lower temperature than freshwater. This is because seawater contains salt. The more salt in the water, the lower its freezing point. Seawater begins freezing at 28°F (−2°C).

The amount of salt in Southern Ocean waters varies. Therefore, the water freezes at different rates. Ice crystals form around areas of saltier water that is not yet cold enough to freeze. These small pockets of water connect to each other, making tiny salt rivers through the ice. The miniature rivers are called brine channels.

As seawater freezes, it forms large pancake-shaped pieces of ice called floes. Ice floes are filled with brine channels. The floes eventually freeze together to make solid ice.

As sea ice forms, ice crystals sometimes grow together in what is known as "pancake ice." The ice floes pictured here are about 3 feet (1 meter) across.

Solid ice is weak where floes are joined. Winds and currents sometimes push them over or under one another. This makes the sea-ice surface rough. Waves and currents make the bottom of the ice rough, too.

Chapter 4

LIFE
in the
SOUTHERN OCEAN

The Southern Ocean is full of life. Many of its plants and animals live on or near the ice. Some even live in it. Southern plants and animals create many different ecosystems. An ecosystem is a group of plants and animals that need each other to survive.

Plankton

Plankton are plants and animals that float about with ocean waves and currents. They live in open water and on the seafloor. Some even live in brine channels or on the bottom of sea ice. Some plankton is so small it can only be seen with a microscope. Other plankton is quite large.

There are two types of plankton. Phytoplankton are plants. Zooplankton are animals.

Krill

The most abundant zooplankton in the Southern Ocean is krill. Krill look like shrimp. The largest

A microscope photo shows a close view of phytoplankton.

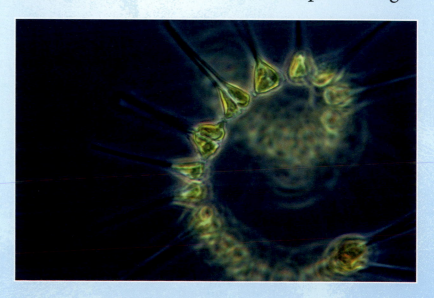

Animal plankton are called zooplankton. The most abundant zooplankton in the Southern Ocean is krill.

ones grow about as long as a person's finger. They are pinkish-red with big black eyes.

In the spring and summer, Southern waters are thick with krill. Thousands of mammals, birds, and fish come to the ocean just to eat them.

Fish

There are about 120 different species of fish in the Southern Ocean. Most live on or near the seafloor. These fish are known as bottom dwellers. Bottom-dwelling fish eat dead plants and animals that sink down to them from above.

LIFE IN THE SOUTHERN OCEAN

Other Deep-Sea Dwellers

Other animals also live in the deep waters of the Southern Ocean. Sea urchins, starfish, and worms live near the ocean bottom. Some actually live in the mud or sand of the seafloor. They, too, eat decaying matter that falls from above.

At an aquarium at McMurdo Station, a scientist looks on at a large Antarctic cod. These fish are one of about 120 different species of fish in the Southern Ocean. The scientists are studying how the fish keep their blood from freezing in the 28°F (−2°C) water.

In addition, about seventy different kinds of squid live in the Southern Ocean. Squid are similar to octopuses, but have eight long arms and two tentacles. They capture prey with suction disks that line their arms and tentacles.

As squid grow older, they live in deeper and deeper waters. The large

squid of the deep waters are an important food source for seals and whales.

Toothed Whales

Several kinds of toothed whales live in the Southern Ocean, including the sperm, Southern bottlenose, and orca whales. Many are migrators that live in the Southern during the summer, then swim to warmer waters for the rest of the year. Toothed whales have teeth for catching and eating food.

Many orca whales stay in the Southern Ocean all year. Orcas eat penguins, seals, and fish.

An orca whale comes up through the ice for air. Orcas are one of many types of whales that swim the waters of the Southern Ocean.

Leopard seals have "leopard" spots on the throat, shoulders, and sides.

They often work together while hunting. For instance, one orca may tip a small iceberg while a waiting orca attacks the seals that fall from it.

Baleen Whales

Baleen whales also live in the Southern Ocean. These whales do not have teeth. They trap food in bristly bones that hang from their jaws. These bones are called baleen. Some baleen whales are also migrators. One, the blue whale, is the largest animal on earth. It can grow to 100 feet (30 meters) long.

Seals

Seals live in the Southern Ocean year round.
They hunt from sea ice. They also use the ice
to rest, give birth, and escape predators.

One common seal of the Southern is the
Weddell. Weddell seals grow to 10 feet
(3 meters) long. They live where there is always
ice. They chop holes in the ice with their teeth
to get into and out of the water. Weddells eat fish,
squid, and krill.

Leopard seals also live in the Southern.
They can grow to 13 feet (4 meters) long.
They are slender and have smooth, dark fur
with light spots. They eat krill, penguins, and
other small seals.

Penguins

Many kinds of penguins live around the Southern
Ocean. Penguins are birds, but they cannot fly.
They use their wings as flippers, and they are
expert swimmers. On land they waddle around
on their tough feet. Penguins eat krill and fish.

The emperor penguin is one species of penguin that lives in the Southern Ocean region.

Adélie penguins are the most numerous penguins in the Southern. They are only 28 inches (71 centimeters) tall.

Emperor penguins are the largest penguins. They stand up to 4 feet (1.2 meters) high. Each year the female lays an egg, then leaves to live in open water.

The male stays back to care for the egg. He lifts it onto his feet and covers it with a thick layer of skin that hangs from his stomach. Then he huddles with hundreds of other males who are also warming their eggs. After three months, the female emperor returns. She finds her mate and waits for the baby to hatch.

Seabirds

Other birds also live around the Southern Ocean. Many come to the ice edge to feed and rest.

The most common bird of the Southern Ocean is the brown skua. Another Southern Ocean bird is the snow petrel. It flies over the water and swoops down to eat zooplankton.

Chapter 5

SOUTHERN EXPLORATION

For centuries, people believed there was a continent at the bottom of the earth. In 1772, a British naval officer named James Cook set out to find it.

Captain Cook

Cook sailed as far south as he could. Then he began a journey around the globe, turning south whenever he found ice-free water.

Cook never saw Antarctica, but he was the first to cross the Antarctic Circle. When he returned to Great Britain, he reported that the waters in the south were filled with whales and seals.

Sealers

Soon seal hunters were headed south. During the first part of the 1800s, hunters killed thousands of Southern Ocean seals each year.

Early Explorers

While sealers hunted, others sailors explored the ocean. Russian explorer Fabian Gottlieb von Bellingshausen was the first to sight Antarctica, in 1820. Ice kept him from getting to the continent, though.

In 1841, James Clark Ross of Great Britain discovered the world's largest body of fast ice. It is now known as the Ross Ice Shelf. The ice gave people a way to get onto Antarctica.

James Cook is known as the first sailor to have navigated the Southern Ocean. Cook and his crew learned a lot about the water at the southern end of the earth.

British naval officer Robert Falcon Scott led two expeditions to the Antarctic: one from 1901 to 1904, and one from 1910 to 1913. Scott's party of five reached the South Pole on January 17, 1912, only to find that Roald Amundsen's Norwegian expedition had beaten them to the glory. On their way back, just 11 miles (18 kilometers) shy of a supply depot, Scott and his men died of starvation and exhaustion.

IN MEMORY OF THE ANTARCTIC HEROES, THE LATE CAPTAIN SCOTT AND HIS GALLANT COMRADES, WHO PERISHED MARCH, 1912, AT THE SOUTH POLE.

Beyond the track of human life,
    Away through an endless waste,
The end achieved, but lo ! sad news
    Of death most bravely faced.

Beyond the woes of earthly strife,
    Away to an endless rest—
A destiny we may not choose
    Has done it's worst, and best.

7199.C ROTARY PHOTO.E.C.

British naval officer Robert Falcon Scott led the first expedition onto Antarctica in 1901. In 1911, Norwegian explorer Roald Amundsen was the first to reach the South Pole.

Sharing for Science

By 1957, several countries had built science bases on Antarctica. The United States was one of them.

It was soon clear to scientists that Antarctica was special. It was the only land on Earth that was

On December 14, 1911, Norwegian explorer Roald Amundsen (right) became the first person to reach the South Pole.

not divided into countries. Many of its natural resources were still untouched. Scientists feared all of this could change.

Their concern led to the writing of the Antarctic Treaty. It said that Antarctica and the Southern Ocean would only be used for peaceful purposes. The polar area would become a giant science laboratory where people from all over the world could study.

Study of the Ocean

Hundreds of scientists did come to study the ocean. Some flew to research stations on land, and then traveled by helicopter or airplane to remote ice floes. Others worked from ships. Often these ships sailed behind icebreakers, vessels built to break through thick ice.

Current Research Stations

The Southern Ocean is still studied today. McMurdo Station is the largest research base on Antarctica. More than one thousand people stay there each summer.

Ships still study the Southern. The *Polarstern* is an icebreaker that takes scientists and equipment to places that have never been studied before. One recent expedition found more than 700 new species in the Southern, showing that there is still much to be learned about this unique body of water.

The OCEAN and the EARTH

The Southern Ocean is one of the most protected areas of the natural world. Even so, the ocean is not completely healthy.

Global Warming

One of the biggest threats to the ocean is climate change. Temperatures around the world are rising, a condition known as global warming. Warmer temperatures are

An iceberg heads north through the Southern Ocean toward Chile.

melting Southern Ocean ice. This is affecting many ecosystems.

Plants and animals that live on, in, and under the ice are losing their homes and dying. This leaves the animals that eat them without food. Eventually these animals will starve. Then the animals that eat them will go hungry. Soon many of them will die. Warming temperatures may even lead to the extinction of some species.

Ozone

Another problem facing the Southern Ocean is the disappearance of the ozone layer. Ozone is a kind of oxygen that surrounds the earth in a covering called the ozone layer.

The ozone layer protects all life from the sun's ultraviolet (UV) rays. Without ozone, radiation from UV rays would kill many forms of life.

During the last half of the twentieth century, chemicals called chlorofluorocarbons (CFCs)

were used in many everyday products. In the late 1980s, scientists discovered that CFCs were destroying the ozone layer. The worst destruction was over Antarctica.

During some parts of the year, nearly half of the ozone layer is missing over Antarctica. It leaves what is known as the ozone hole. In 2010, the Antarctic ozone hole was over 8 million square miles (22 million square kilometers). Experts believe that some Southern Ocean plankton has already died from the increase in UV rays.

During the 1990s, several nations stopped using CFCs. This has helped some, but other chemicals that harm the ozone are still in use.

Hunting

Another problem facing the Southern Ocean is overhunting. Seals were nearly hunted to extinction in the 1800s. Once the hunting was stopped, their populations began to recover. Today there are thousands of seals living in the Southern Ocean.

The nations that do research in Antarctica and throughout the Southern Ocean have agreed to try to protect the area's pristine beauty.

Southern Ocean whales have also been overhunted. During the late 1990s, several countries agreed to stop almost all whale hunting. Unfortunately, protection for whales may have come too late. Several Southern Ocean whales are endangered, including the blue and humpback whales.

Overfishing

Overfishing is also harming the Southern. This means fish are being caught faster than they are able to reproduce. Overfishing can lead to a species becoming extinct.

The Patagonian toothfish is in danger of being overfished. It is often caught by longline fishing. Longline fishing creates another kind of problem. The long lines and hooks used on longlines often kill seabirds, too.

Land of Peace

Antarctica and the Southern Ocean are the only places on earth where the world's most powerful nations have agreed to maintain peace. People are also trying to make it a place where nature can be left in peace.

SOUTHERN OCEAN FACTS

✓ **Area**
About 7,848,000 square miles (20,327,000 square kilometers)

✓ **Average Depth**
13,100 to 16,400 feet (4,000 to 5,000 meters)

✓ **Greatest Known Depth**
South Sandwich Trench 23,736 feet (7,235 meters)

✓ **Surface Temperature**
The temperature is almost always the same, around 28°F (−2°C).

✓ **Other Names**
Some people refer to the Southern Ocean as the Antarctic Ocean. Some scientists feel that the Southern Ocean is part of the Atlantic, Pacific, and Indian oceans. In 2000, the International Hydrographic Organization made the existence of the Southern Ocean official.

WORDS TO KNOW

basin—In the ocean, a large bowl-shaped area that is deeper than the surrounding area; basins often have a sandy bottom.

brine channel—One of the tiny salt rivers that flow through the sea ice.

circumpolar—Surrounding or going around one of Earth's poles.

climate—The general weather patterns of a particular area.

continental shelf—The submerged border of a large landmass.

continental slope—The part of the continental shelf that drops off steeply to the ocean floor.

current—A strong movement of water in one direction.

glacier—A large body of ice that moves slowly over land.

global warming—Climate change that causes temperatures to rise, which will in turn make it harder for some types of plants and animals to survive.

iceberg—A large floating piece of ice that has broken off a glacier.

ice floe—A large floating piece of ice that forms on the surface of the sea.

krill—Tiny shelled animals that make up the plankton on which whales feed.

McMurdo Station—A research center on the shore of McMurdo Sound in Antarctica.

mid-ocean ridge—The underwater mountain range that runs through all the oceans of the world.

ocean—The entire body of salt water that covers most of the earth, including the Atlantic Ocean, Pacific Ocean, Indian Ocean, Arctic Ocean, and Southern Ocean.

oceanographer—A scientist who studies the ocean.

overfishing—The act of fishing so often in one area or for one type of fish that very few fish are left to continue the cycle of life.

ozone layer—A layer of atmosphere about 20 miles (32 kilometers) above Earth that protects Earth's surface from harmful sunrays.

penguin—Any of the short-legged seabirds that live around the Southern Ocean; penguins cannot fly but use their wings as flippers for swimming.

phytoplankton—Plant plankton.

plankton—Mostly tiny plants and animals, phytoplankton and zooplankton, that float in the water.

Polarstern—The name of a large ship that can break through the ice; it also carries scientists and their research equipment.

research station—A laboratory and living quarters set up for scientists to use when they study hard-to-reach places, such as Antarctica.

resource—Anything that can be used as a source of energy, a supply, or a support, such as oil or gas, sand, or food.

sea ice—Frozen seawater.

seal—A sea-dwelling mammal that lives mostly in cold regions, feeds especially on fish, and uses short flippers to swim and dive.

sea urchin—An animal that lives on the seafloor and has a roundish shell covered with spines that can move.

squid—A sea-dwelling animal that has a thin shell inside its long, soft body and eight short arms plus two longer tentacles.

starfish—A sea-dwelling animal that has a skeleton, but no backbone, and many arms arranged around a center.

treaty—An agreement made by and between countries.

trench—A deep gash in the ocean floor.

whale—A very large sea-dwelling mammal that breathes air through a hole on the top of its head.

zooplankton—Animal plankton.

BOOKS

Bateman, Robert, and Nancy Kovacs. *Polar Worlds: Life at the Ends of the Earth.* Toronto: Scholastic/Madison Press, 2008.

Green, Jen. *Frozen Extremes.* New York: Crabtree Publishing, 2009.

Kalman, Bobbie, and Rebecca Sjonger. *Explore Antarctica.* St. Catherines, ON: Crabtree Publishing, 2007.

Schaefer, A. R. *Spotlight on Antarctica.* Mankato, Minn.: Capstone Press, 2011.

WEB SITES

National Geographic Photo Gallery. *Animals of Antarctica.* <http://animals.nationalgeographic.com/animals/photos/antarctic-animals>

NOAA for Kids. <http://oceanservice.noaa.gov/kids>

INDEX